WINNIPEG
WALKS
by
The Prairie Pathfinders

Winnipeg Walks

Copyright ©2004 Prairie Pathfinders Inc.

The authors of this material shall not be held responsible for any injury, losses, damages, expenses, or fines that may result through the use of this guide, and urge readers to exercise all reasonable precautions.

Published by Prairie Pathfinders Inc.
PO Box 68052
RPO Osborne Village
Winnipeg, Manitoba, Canada R3L 2V9

Printed in Canada by Friesens

Second Edition
ISNB 0-9683976-3-8

Canadian Cataloguing In Publication Data
Main entry under title:

Winnipeg walks

ISBN 0-9683976-3-8

1. Walking--Manitoba--Winnipeg--Guidebooks.
2. Winnipeg (Man.)--Tours. I. Prairie Pathfinders (Association).

FC3396.18.W55 1998   917.127'4304   C98-920131-7
F1064.5.W7W55 1998

A grant from the Winnipeg Foundation, a contributor to the quality of life in our community since 1921, helped make this publication possible. We also gratefully acknowledge the sponsorship of Heritage Winnipeg, the City of Winnipeg - Parks and Open Space Division, and a generous financial contribution from Harvey Smith, Councillor for Daniel McIntyre Ward.

Introduction

Winnipeg Walks is intended for those who love walking as well as those who take delight in exploring. If you can walk a trail, however slowly, this guide will open up a treasure trove of Winnipeg's scenic delights. It also throws in a crash course on some of our more colourful history. Most of all this is a terrific guide for discovering Winnipeg's different neighbourhoods.

Learning about and appreciating a place, is best done on foot. If you really want to see Winnipeg - its wonderful urban forest, its stately old residential areas, its impressive architecture, its beautiful park trails - you have to get out and walk around it - witness it firsthand.

This book describes thirty-eight of the best walks - sidewalk routes, trails, and parkway paths - in and around Winnipeg. You'll discover the beauty of an abandoned rail line in Charleswood and the charm of worker cottages in Point Douglas. You'll find lots of surprises including a terrific system of linear parkways along our rivers and streams. Hopefully you'll also find that walking is an excellent way to have fun while you're keeping fit.

The Prairie Pathfinders first published this guide in September 1998. Since that time it has sold 10,000 copies (making it a Canadian best seller - three times over). The Prairie Pathfinders Walking Club which was established as a complement to the book, has now grown to include more than 500 members and holds hundreds of guided walks in Winnipeg every year.

Prairie Pathfinders Inc. is a non profit group originated by four women (Leone Banks, Kathleen Leathers, Sheila Spence and Wendy Wilson) who have as their primary goal the promotion of walking and hiking in Manitoba and making Winnipeg truly a 'walkers' city'.

Please visit our Website at:
www.prairiepathfinders.mb.ca

City Centre

St Boniface

North Winnipeg

Northeast Winnipeg

South Winnipeg

Southwest Winnipeg

West Winnipeg

Outside the perimeter

Winter only hikes

Start The Forks
Distance 5.5 km loop

This circle route takes you through the historic heart of Winnipeg and begins at **The Forks** - the centre of our city in so many ways.

The importance of this famous junction of the Red and Assiniboine rivers can be traced back 6000 years when it served as an assembly point for the aboriginal people. It was a critical link in the western fur trade and European settlement, and later, a major debarkation point for immigrants to western Canada. Sadly this area lay neglected and deserted for more than half a century. But its value to us has finally come full circle. With the award winning Forks development, the juncture where the Assiniboine River flows into the Red is once again our pre-eminent gathering place.

For walking enthusiasts, The Forks is heaven-sent. Beautifully

designed trails, riverwalk paths and foot bridges link The Forks with the rest of the city and make walking to it a perfectly grand experience. When you factor in the many outdoor festivities and celebrations, the unique shops and eateries, as well as exciting new and heritage architecture on these beautifully landscaped grounds, The

Forks, becomes a wonderful "destination walk". All pathways are well lit and well maintained and apart from the spring flood water, provide great walking all year round.

Begin at The Forks site and walk down the steps to the marina, then turn right and follow the Assiniboine Riverwalk. Pass under the bridge then climb the stone steps to

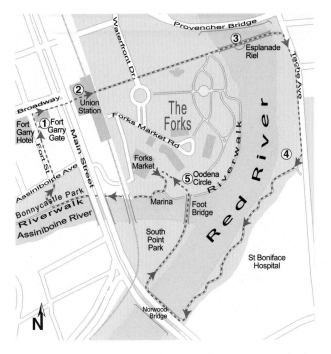

Bonnycastle Park. Cross Assiniboine Ave and walk north along Fort Street. On your left you'll see the beautiful Hotel Fort Garry and on your right the site of historic Upper Fort Garry.

1 This little park that contains the stone **Fort Garry Gate** is all that remains of that famous fort. Colourful plaques and panels explain the history of Upper Fort Garry and its significance in the beginnings of the City of Winnipeg.

Walk out to either Main Street or Broadway Avenue, then to Union Station where you'll walk in the front entrance and straight through to the rear exit.

2 **Union Station** is an architectural gem and well worth a quick tour. This imposing structure shared the same design team with the famous Grand Central Station in New York city. Be sure to look up at the beautiful domed ceiling as you pass through.

historical markers and offers an excellent view of The Forks across the river.

Cross the parking lot and follow a well landscaped path toward Winnipeg's newest landmark - the famous Esplanade Riel.

3 Esplanade Riel - Love it or hate it, your attention is definitely drawn to the dramatic design of this new pedestrian bridge. Controversy aside, the eye-catching structure seems to be a crowd-pleaser and is clearly attracting a lot of foot traffic.

After you cross the 'ped bridge', turn right and proceed south down Tache Avenue. When you near St Boniface Hospital, turn into the Grey Nuns Walkway - a winding asphalt path along the river behind the hospital complex. This path is dotted with

4 Grey Nuns Walkway - In 1844, four Grey Nuns from Montreal landed on these banks. It had been a long and difficult journey - 59 days by canoe. They had come to teach, but soon realized they were needed far more as nurses. They set up an infirmary and over the next 10 years made thousands of calls to the tents and shanties, ministering to the sick. In 1871, the Grey Nuns founded St. Boniface General Hospital - now one of the largest and most respected research and teaching health centres in western Canada.

This walkway will bring you to the Norwood Bridge. Cross the Red River and find a gravel path leading off to the right through a green space called South Point. You'll reach the Historic Rail Bridge which leads you across the Assiniboine River and back to The Forks and Oodena Circle.

5 **Oodena Circle** - The Celebration Circle is a fascinating place representing harmony with the solar system, wind, earth and water. "Oodena" is an Ojibway word meaning "heart of the community". This outdoor sanctuary with its grassy slopes and sandstone pillars, focuses our attention on the natural cycle of the stars, sun and moon and is aligned to the sunrise and sunset of the fall and spring equinox and the summer and winter solstice. At night, searchlights from within the pillars create teepees in the sky to further direct our attention upwards.

Osborne Village

Start	Legislative Buildings on Broadway Ave
Distance	6.5 km loop
Park	Kennedy Street

This sidewalk route puts the emphasis on fascinating architecture in the centre of the city.

1 The Legislative Building This impressive edifice was constructed of native Tyndall stone quarried east of Selkirk and is an example of neoclassical architecture on a grand scale. The magnificent Golden Boy that tops the dome is 16 feet from toe to torch and is sheathed in 24 karat gold. The torch in his right hand points to progress and economic development and the sheaf of wheat in the left arm represents the agricultural roots on which our province was founded.

2 **Dalnavert** is an example of Queen Anne Revival architecture and is among the last of the many old mansions that once stood in this part of the city. Most have been demolished to make room for office buildings, parking and apartment blocks. It was built in 1895 by the only son of Canada's first Prime Minister - Hugh John Macdonald. The name "Dalnavert" commemorates both his father's home in Toronto and his maternal grandmother's birthplace in Scotland.

As was the fate of other big houses in the Broadway area, Dalnavert was a rooming house from 1929-1969 when the Manitoba Historical Society purchased the house and began restoration

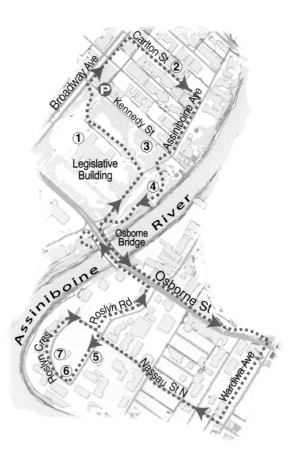

3 **Government House**, on the southeast grounds of the Legislative Building, is a stylish piece of architecture with its wrought iron and mansard roof. It was built in 1883 and is the Queen's

official residence in Manitoba and home of our Lieutenant Governor.

4 The **demonstration gardens** on the Legislative grounds are a great place for gardening enthusiasts to check out different species of plants. Begun in 1997, the head gardener for the province has set up a series of beds on the riverbank for flowers, vegetables, and shrubs. There is also an arboretum with the different trees tagged for identification.

As you cross Osborne Bridge you enter the most densely populated neighbourhood in western Canada. The five blocks of Osborne Street that make up the heart of 'the village' have a vibrancy and a sense of community that are hard to define or understand. A somewhat Bohemian quality pervades this popular commercial and residential area. Perhaps it's left over from the '60s when this was central headquarters for hippie culture.

With the building of the Osborne bridge in 1882 and Winnipeg's first electrified streetcar line in the decade

following, Fort Rouge experienced a boom. Many residents living on Corydon and Gertrude in the early 1880's were engaged in the building trades or the burgeoning railway industry with its major Fort Rouge yards to the south. In the areas closer to the Assiniboine River, lots were larger and the grandest residential structures were found near the bridge.

5 218 Roslyn Road

Passers-by are drawn to the elegant plaster ornamentation of Moss House. With its formal symmetry and handsome proportions, it is surprising to learn that four different architects over a period of 15 years had a hand in its design.

Roslyn Crescent was the site of the great Augustus Nanton estate - one of the grandest houses in Winnipeg. Although the main house was demolished in 1935, the entrance gates, stables and gatehouse remain.

6 "The Cottage" - 229 Roslyn Road

The Nanton Estate Gatehouse may have originally been a gardener's cottage. Built in 1910, it was relocated ten years later to its present site by the front entry gates. During the Depression, it was renovated and expanded, reusing materials such as oak panelling and the Tudor mantel from the demolished mansion. In 1935, the widowed Lady Nanton made this her residence.

7 Nanton House Stables - 61 Roslyn Crescent

The original plan of these Tudor style stables was a U shape building surrounding an open carriage court The buildings were renovated for residential use in 1940, but retained many distinctive elements such as the wooden cupola.

Cornish Path

Start	River path at east end of Cornish
Distance	5 km return
Park	Cornish Avenue

This is a classic urban walk that includes a stretch of trail that's been a Prairie Pathfinder favourite for years. The **Cornish Path** skirts the Assiniboine River between the Osborne Street bridge and Armstrong Point. It winds through some of the most breathtakingly beautiful cottonwood trees in the city and supplies spectacular views - especially of the Legislative Building. It's an informal trail - really a series of monkey trails, and to the uninitiated a truly scenic find. It's also one of the city's most popular corridors for pedestrians and cyclists. It's used by hundreds of people every day through all seasons.

Access the Cornish Path at the east end of Cornish Avenue. This quiet woodlands trail leads you to the Assiniboine River Walk. Proceed under the Obsorne bridge and along the walkway to the Midtown bridge. Cross the river and return down River Avenue and Roslyn Road. Cross the Osborne Bridge, return by the Cornish Path and end with a tour of majestic Armstrong Point.

1 The **Granite Curling Club** at 22 Mostyn Place was designated a heritage building in 1986. Legislative Building architect, James Chisholm, designed this three storey Tudor framed clubhouse, and Thomas Kelly built it in 1909.

2 Our **Legislative Building** displays a wealth of ornamental detail. It's a treat to walk slowly around the periphery of the building and look up. The exceptionally grand interior spaces are worth checking out as well.

3 This 16 foot statue was erected by the Manitoba Metis Foundation to commemorate **Louis Riel**. Riel was a controversial figure whose contribution to Canadian history was much disputed until he was accorded status as the founding father of Manitoba in 1992.

4 Today it's a bit down at the heel but when first built in 1909, **the Roslyn** represented the height of elegant apartment living in Winnipeg.

5 The tyndall stone gates of **Armstrong Point** are a city landmark. They mark the entrance to

Point's location began to attract the attention of Winnipeg's economic elite by the late 1880s and early 1900s when three streets with large lots were laid out down the length of the peninsula.

6 **54 West Gate** was built for Charles Gordon a.k.a. Ralph Connor in 1914. Connor became wealthy writing popular novels such as "Glengarry School Days" and "The Sky Pilot". The house has been the home of the University Women's Club since 1939.

one of the city's oldest neighbourhoods with buildings rich in historic and architectural significance. Armstrong

7 **Eden House** at 147 East Gate was built in 1882 and is the oldest house in the neighbourhood. In earlier days there was a tennis court on the seven acres behind the house which the neighbours called the Bird Cage Club. The property was later divided into three lots and sold.

54 West Gate

| **Start** | The Forks |
| **Distance** | 4.5 km return |

The
Forks

Foot
Bridge

Main Street

Assiniboine River

Norwood
Bridge

Wpg
Rowing
Club

St Marys Rd

Norwood
Community Club

Walmer St

Pinedale

Birchdale

Lawndale

Ferndale

Kirkdale

Red River

Highfield St

Norwood
Flats

Coniston

Lyndale Drive

N

With its beautiful canopy of elm trees and well-kept unpretentious homes, Norwood Flats is like our own Pleasantville. For many years, much of this was a golf course and remained largely undeveloped until after WWII.

Our route originates in The Forks. We first cross the Historic Rail Bridge to South Point then the new Norwood Bridge. Stairs take you down to a walkway that leads under the bridge and onto a path to the Winnipeg Rowing Club and the sunken playing fields of the Norwood Community Club.

The soil was dredged out of this bowl to build up the dyke along Lyndale Drive during the great flood of 1950. Amazingly when so much of the city was under water, this low-lying area successfully escaped the ravages of the flood.

Start The Forks
Distance 8 km return

This walk through Winnipeg's oldest neighbourhood is full of historic and architectural interest, as well as a few surprises. Beginning at the Forks, it offers sweeping riverscapes of old St. Boniface while wending through Juba Park and on past the Alexander Dock.

1 To descend to the River Walk, walk south towards the marina and find the '**Wall of Time**' on your left. Inscriptions on the stone wall gives an account of events at the Forks from prehistory to the fur trade era.

2 A wooden dyke leads to Stephen **Juba Park** - named for one of Winnipeg's more colourful mayors. Bordered by mighty elms and cottonwoods, this park is a welcome splash of green in the downtown area, and stretches from the Provencher Bridge to May Street.

A walkway leads around the Harbour Master headquarters at the end of James Avenue. This is the site referred to when river water levels are recorded in Winnipeg.

3 The 600 foot **Alexander Dock** is the last remnant of commercial shipping on the Red.

From 1859-1876, Point Douglas was the heart of river commerce. Steamboats brought settlers, supplies and construction materials from the United States, and floating department stores on flatbeds would arrive to deal directly with residents.

4 Note the **Scots Monument** erected by the St. Andrews Society on the former site of Fort Douglas. It honours the 400 Selkirk Settlers who arrived between 1812 and 1814 to begin a farming community. Fields to the west, named Colony Gardens by the early settlers, were planted with vegetables and feed grain by the Hudson's Bay Co. to sustain the settlers when they first arrived.

A landscaped gravel path, bordered by a heavy growth of prairie sage and cotton burdock, leads to Curtis Street and a lovely old frame house with a

giant cottonwood in the yard. Most of the homes here are a pleasant surprise. This block is affectionately called "Artland" as many residents are in one way or another connected to the arts scene. Look for some unusual house decoration decisions and interesting sculptures.

Follow Annabella St across to the north side of Point Douglas.

In the early part of the century, this street was famous for bootleg liquor and over 50 brothels.

The first and only Selkirk settlers to farm the point were Kate and Alexander Sutherland. They

built their house where Sutherland Avenue now ends, but the great flood of 1852 carried their log cabin all the way across the river to St. Boniface. Rather than build anew, they purchased land there and became neighbours of the Lagimodieres and the Riels. Perhaps as a result, their only child John came to speak French and Cree and later was an important peacemaker between the Metis and the settlers during the 1869-70 Red River rebellion.

In the early part of this century, Point Douglas was distinctly rural. Everyone kept a cow and chickens. You may eye a garage or outer building with an odd appearance, and that will no doubt be because it started out as a horse barn.

At the north end of Stephens St. stands a giant cottonwood which may be 180-200 years old and is the largest tree in downtown Winnipeg. It was growing on the banks of the Red River when the Selkirk Settlers arrived.

Point Douglas was to become Winnipeg's first elite neighbourhood. Dry goods agent E.L. Barber's house, built in 1867, is the oldest house still standing in the city. The Ashdown home, which used to stand at 109 Euclid, was an example of the mansions built by later arrivals in the neighbourhood and were in marked contrast to the simple Barber house. In 1877 J.H. Ashdown built a substantial three storey brick house with furnace and

indoor plumbing. It was complete with circular driveway, flower beds and furniture imported from Minnesota.

5 As you look around from Joe Zuken Heritage Park you have a real sense of the age of the neighbourhood. **Ross House**, Winnipeg's first post office, is a prime example of Red River construction and was made almost entirely of hand carved log timber.

The first train steamed over the Louise bridge and west along the length of Point Douglas in July 1881. The arrival of that first train marked a watershed for the neighbourhood. It meant railway yards, industry, noise, smell and smoke. The genteel tranquillity that had lured Winnipeg's upper crust soon vanished. Mansions and lots were subdivided and small working class houses were crowded in beside faded mansions.

Start	The Forks
Distance	4 km return

Winnipeg's Exchange District is bursting with one of the most dazzling collections of turn-of-the-last-century architecture in North America. Massive Greek columns, elaborate facades, and gargoyles tell the story of our illustrious economic past.

Between 1880 and 1920, 'Chicago of the North' Winnipeg, was a dominate force in western Canada. This was the city's distribution and immigration hub - home to a vibrant financial industry, the world's busiest grain exchange, plus thousands of warehouse and manufacturing enterprises.

The architectural character of the District draws from the Chicago style and includes Victorian, Romanesque and Edwardian influences. Designed by a number of well known architects, the buildings of the Exchange District reflect an approach to architecture

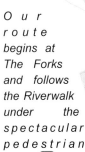

This walk serves as an introductory or 'mini' tour past some of the more eye-catching buildings. For a an up-close look at this fabulous architecture, you can join one of the guided historic walking tours held daily throughout the summer months.

that was innovative and stylish. The First World War, the opening of the Panama Canal and the Great Depression contributed to the end of Winnipeg's spectacular boom era but luckily the district remained virtually intact. Through the efforts of dedicated citizens, the Exchange District architecture has been preserved as a distinctive legacy and is now a national historic site.

Today the banks and warehouses have given way to bars and restaurants. The cobble stone sidewalks are dotted with stylish art galleries and a shopper's paradise for antiques and vintage clothing.

Our route begins at The Forks and follows the Riverwalk under the spectacular pedestrian bridge **1** **Esplanade Riel** *and under the Provencher Bridge to a path that runs parallel to Waterfront Drive (our city's newest scenic roadway) and* **2** *past our popular* **baseball park**.

3 **Old Market Square** found in the heart of the district is the hub of the city's visual arts community and in summer, the centre of Winnipeg's famous Fringe Festival.

4 On the return loop through Juba Park, consider hailing a **water taxi** back to The Forks.

Start	Trail behind Fort Gibraltar in Whittier Park
Distance	5.5 km loop
Parking	Parking lot south of the Fort

Our route follows the Red River through a strip of river-bottom forest to the mouth of the Seine, then south under a railway bridge to a walking bridge over the Seine. Cross and turn left down a set of wooden steps to a landscaped river bank walkway. Return on city streets.

Whittier Park was a race track from the 1880s until 1925. The Park is named for poet John Greenleaf Whittier who paid homage to the St. Boniface Cathedral in the 1850s with the words, "The bells of the Roman Mission, That call from their turrets twain, To the boatman on the river - To the hunter on the plain."

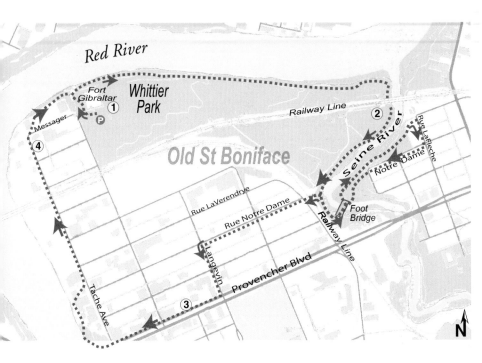

Whittier Park comes alive each February during the Festival du Voyageur - when the restored **Fort Gibraltar** is open to the public. The original Fort was built in 1807 by the North West Fur Company. It was their halfway house on the 3000 mile fur route to Montreal. The week long Festival brings Manitoba's French and fur trade heritage to the forefront.

An explorer in 1801 reported on an abundance of huge trees in this area - elm, basswood, poplar and oak so tall that their branches started 50 feet up the trunk. By 1890 this area was completely denuded, as settlers had cut down all trees for building and firewood.

1 One elm survived. It is about 10 metres from the south turret of reconstructed Fort Gibraltar and is believed to be over 260 years old. This heritage **Whittier Park elm** is 4 metres in circumference, 26 metres tall, and beautifully shaped.

The flood plain along the Red and Seine rivers is covered with thick layers of alluvial soil. Scars on the tree trunks show where ice jams have gouged the trees during spring floods, and refuse stuck in the branches evidence the height of the 1997 flood.

2 Jean Baptiste and Marie Anne **Lagimodiere**, the first farmers in St. Boniface, built a log cabin here on the banks of the Seine in 1819. Lagimodiere is a legendary

figure for his celebrated 5 month walk from Winnipeg to Montreal, carrying a plea for help from the Red River settlers to Lord Selkirk. As a result, he was awarded most of the land in this area including Whittier Park. Marie Anne is also the stuff of legends. She arrived here by canoe in 1806 and was the first white woman west of Lake Superior. Her first child, Julia, was born in 1807 in a wigwam pitched on the banks of the Pembina River south of Winnipeg. Julia was to become the mother of Louis Riel.

3 As you turn onto **Provencher** you enter the real heart of the French Quarter. This grand tree lined boulevard is undergoing something of a renaissance with the completion of our new foot bridge (Esplanade Riel) introducing a wealth of foot traffic to the shops and eateries of Old St Boniface.

4 If you glance to your right as you reach the end of Tache you'll catch sight of an unusual part of our city's infrastructure that is also an unusually attractive piece of architecture. This brick tower is one half of the 'Tache Booster Pumping Station' and although built in 1918, it still has a functional role in our city's water system. During periods when water demand is high, this station increases the flow of water to our in-town reservoir and the tower protects the aqueduct against pressure surges.

Start	Franco Manitoban Centre - 340 Provencher
Distance	6.5 km
Parking	Franco Manitoban Centre parking lot

This walk is through some of the city's most important cultural landmarks. Discover an interesting mix of architectural styles and enjoy some fine views of the Seine River.

From the Franco-Manitoban Centre, proceed east along Provencher Blvd, crossing DesMeurons, until you reach the Seine River. On your right, find the Seine River Interpretive Trail. This trail will take you south almost as far as Goulet Street. From that point, you will return to a sidewalk route around the central area of Saint Boniface.

There has been a French presence in this area since Quebec fur traders arrived in the mid 1700s. Voyageurs working for the North West Company settled in what is now St. Boniface with their native born wives. These French voyageurs fathered a new French speaking Catholic nation - the Metis.

After the clash between the Metis and the Selkirk Settlers in 1817, Lord Selkirk attempted to resolve the conflict by requesting the Roman Catholic church send missionaries from Quebec. He believed that the church would provide stability to the French-Catholic settlement. To encourage them to locate on the east side of the Red River, he granted the Catholic church a large plot of land there. In 1819 a small chapel was built. Most of the elements which shaped St. Boniface's character were in place by the early 1830s. The farm lots occupied by French Catholic settlers reached from the mouth of the Seine to the LaSalle River and beyond. Their community life centered upon the institutions and works of the St. Boniface mission - the centre and symbol of French Manitoba.

1 **La Vielle Gare** - 630 Des Meurons. Now a fine French restaurant, this lovely railway station, built of bricks imported from Missouri, served the people of southeast Manitoba for many years before becoming obsolete.

3 **King Edward School** - 261 Youville. Built as a public school in 1915, it is a fine example of school architecture of that period. It is now a designated

2 **The Roy House** - 375 Rue Deschambault
The childhood home of Gabrielle Roy, one of Canada's most distinguished writers and author of fifteen books, including The Tin Flute, The Road Past Altamont and The Street of Riches, which describes her family's life on Rue Deschambault.

historic building and home to The Springs Christian Academy.

4 **Enfield Crescent** is a true crescent. At one time it skirted an oxbow of the Red River, and the slope of the ancient riverbank is still obvious. As the Red wanders across its plain, large loops evolve, similar to the one around Point Douglas. Oxbows are created as erosion cuts away at the base of the peninsula. Eventually the river cuts through a new channel, and the old river bed becomes

Kenny Street near the junction of the rear lane of Kitson Street. This elm figured prominently in the life of a well known young pioneer named Victor Mager. Mager had moved with his family from Lorraine, France, in 1859 to take residence near the present site of St. Boniface Hospital. In the early years, Mr. Mager regularly hunted wild game throughout the areas now referred to as Norwood and St. Vital. On one of his forays in 1889, he marked the tree with a cross, and it soon became a recognized landmark. The tree is still in good condition and is about 70 feet high.

isolated, fills with silt, and becomes a marsh. The Enfield marsh appeared on maps prior to 1900.

5 Precious Blood Church

- 200 Kenny Street Designed by local architect Etienne Gaboury, the spiral form imitates the "teepee" of the prairies. Both exterior and interior are unique in terms of church architecture and well worth a tour.

6 Locally named the "**Kenny Street Elm**", this historic elm is located on the west boulevard of

7 Saint Boniface Museum

- 494 Tache Avenue. Originally a convent for the Grey Nuns, who arrived from Montreal in 1844, this national historic site built in 1846 is the oldest building in the city and the largest oak log construction in North America.

8 Saint Boniface Cathedral

- 190 Cathedral Avenue. The Basilica built in 1908 was destroyed by fire in 1968. The

Roy House

present structure, designed by Etienne Gaboury, incorporates the remaining Romanesque facade, arches, pillars and statue of Saint Boniface. In the cemetery you will find the final resting place of Louis Riel, recognised in 1992, as the founder of Manitoba.

9 Archbishop's Palace - 141 Cathedral Avenue. The western portion of the palace was built in 1864 and is one of the oldest stone structures still standing in western Canada. Note the elegant Mansard roof.

10 Saint Boniface College - 200 Cathedral Avenue. The College's tradition of French education dates back to 1818. It now offers French study bachelor degrees in Arts, Science, Education and Translation.

11 Provencher School - 320 Cathedral Avenue. The origin of the Provencher Institute for boys dates back to the arrival of Father Provencher. The location of the school changed three times before it finally resided in the present building, and it was not until 1968 that the school began to teach both boys and girls.

Start	Kildonan Park
Distance	8.5 km return
Parking	Pavilion parking lot

This is a walk straight through the early history of our city. Beginning in carefully manicured Kildonan Park, our route takes you down Scotia Street, south towards the onion domes of Holy Trinity Cathedral and ends at historic St. John's Cathedral Cemetery near Winnipeg's oldest park.

1 Kildonan Park - One of the most striking things about this park is the lovely creek with its footbridges and rolling terrain. The gravel paths and roadway circling the English Landscape design of this park are popular with walkers year round. Other features such as the outdoor theatre, swimming pool, brilliant formal flower gardens and massive trees make this a jewel in Winnipeg's park system.

West Kildonan was the first agricultural settlement in western Canada. Between 1812 and 1814, sixty families were brought over from Scotland by Lord Selkirk. They settled on this side of the river because it was free of heavy timber having been burned over some years earlier. This saved them the back breaking labour of clearing the land before plowing it to seed their crops. The farms were long narrow lots having river frontage of 330 -660 feet, and running two miles back from the river with another two mile 'hay privilege' beyond. The river frontage varied in accordance with the number of children in the family, with 66 additional feet given for each child.

Scotia Street was named for Old Scotia, Scotland, home of many of these settlers. It was originally a walking path that connected their rough log dwellings with a trading post in Point Douglas.

2 **Seven Oaks House** at 115 Rupertsland takes its name from a nearby creek where seven oaks once stood, also marking the site of the battle of that name. It was built in the 1850s by John Inkster, a Hudson's Bay man born in the Orkney Isles in 1799. He arrived in the settlement in 1824 and married Mary Sinclair (daughter of a Hudson's Bay Factor and a Cree mother). Mary was 'good with figures' and managed their store while John handled their other interests. John built this nine room house after establishing himself here as a prosperous farmer, free trader and merchant. He did part of the building himself, including the stone foundation which withstood the disastrous flood of 1852 when most other buildings in the area were washed away. It was constructed of oak logs which were floated down the Assiniboine & Red from Baie St. Paul (near Portage La Prairie). The shingles

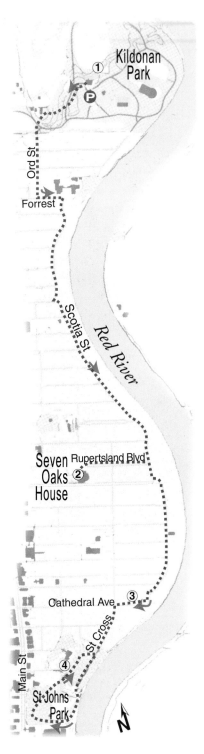

4 The graveyard around **St. John's Cathedral** is older than the church, and was used as early as 1812 by Selkirk Settlers. By the south east corner of the Cathedral an unusual piece of history is recorded on a pink granite monument. The inscription reads "Sacred to the memory of my mother, Margaret Sinclair. This last token of love and affection is erected by her wandering boy Colin", the same Capt. Sinclair who slept in a hammock in Seven Oaks House. He was 81 when

were handmade of cedar and the glass. paint, putty, door locks, hinges, and nails were all brought out from England.

One second floor bedroom belonged to Captain Colin Sinclair, who was Mary Inkster's brother. He settled here after more than 60 years at sea and refused to use a bed. He continued to sleep in his beloved hammock until he died in 1901. Today the hammock still hangs from its original hooks.

3 An **historic tree** with an arresting appearance stands at 57 Cathedral. The story goes that in 1851 it was used as a pulpit by our first Presbyterian minister, John Black, before he had a church. It is a Manitoba maple, usually upright and bushy, but it grew too close to a log cabin (long vanished) and its branches twisted to find the sun.

he had this inscribed, and had at last returned to his birthplace, seventy two years after he had left. In 1825 as a boy of nine, while visiting on a ship docked at Fort Prince of Wales, he fell asleep, and the Ship's Captain sailed away taking Colin to Scotland to be educated (as his dead father had wished). This was done without Colin's mother's knowledge or consent, and she never saw him again. From Scotland Colin set out for a life at sea. But his attachment to his dead mother, to whom he hadn't

said good-bye those many years before, brought him back for this final act of homage.

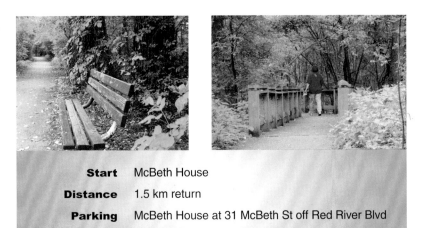

Start	McBeth House
Distance	1.5 km return
Parking	McBeth House at 31 McBeth St off Red River Blvd

To reach the park drive north on Main Street past the Chief Peguis Bridge and turn right onto Red River Blvd then left on McBeth Street. The walk begins at McBeth House.

Alexander McBeth first settled this land in 1815 and his descendants lived here until 1976. In that year his family made a gift of the property to the city for a park.

This is a short and pleasant trail through lovely green space bordering the upscale suburb of Rivergrove. It has the added virtue of being completely accessible for wheelchair and child stroller.

The asphalt path winds first through a tall grass prairie restoration site and then through a beautiful river bottom forest that has some of Winnipeg's largest cottonwood trees.

Start	Gunn Rd park entrance
Distance	1 km loop
Parking	Parking lot on Gunn Rd

This bioreserve represents a 'good news' story about how a neighbourhood had an adjoining property transformed from a polluted industrial site to a pleasant public park.

This was a Domtar wood-preserving plant for the better part of the last century and over time it became contaminated with hazardous waste. In 1998, the province negotiated with the company to clean up the property. What was at issue, however, was how exactly that would be accomplished. After many meetings and consultations and involvement from the community, an imaginative plan was conceived. Domtar was to scrape up all polluted soil, contain it on site in a cell and cover it with a grassy berm. The remainder of the property would be rehabilitated as a natural park. It was a 'win win' situation. Domtar was saved the cost of hauling away all contaminates and Transcona residents gained access to a new park.

Part of the deal negotiated gave development and management of this bioreserve to the Fort Whyte Centre.

At present the park landscape is somewhat stark. Over time it will be instructive to see how successfully native plantings return.

Bunn's Creek

Start	Henderson Hwy
Distance	5 km return
Parking	Parking lot on west side of Henderson Hwy near Knowles

This gravel path along Bunn's Creek takes you from Henderson Highway to McIvor Avenue, through a beautifully natural linear parkway.

Our path follows the creek as it meanders through 23 acres of park. Bunn's Creek Park provides the surrounding community of River East (a mix of large contemporary homes and older bungalows) with a country like atmosphere and is an ideal setting for a recreational foot path.

North Kildonan remained outside the area of intense urban settlement until the early 1970s. By this time the city's parks department was becoming interested in developing green spaces with wild or natural vegetation intact. Bunn's Creek as a 'natural' park is now a perfect model for the rest of the city.

The many lovely gardens that back onto the parkway are themselves worth the trip. One has been featured in a number of garden magazines.

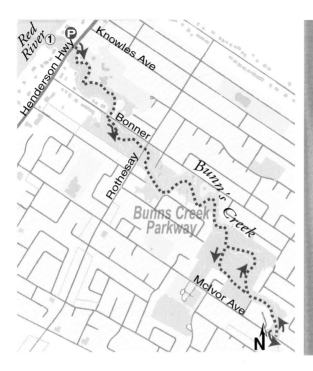

1 side trip

At the parking lot on the west side of Henderson Highway, a winding path takes you to forks of the Red River and Bunn's Creek and a view across the Red of McBeth Park and a stand of Plains cottonwood that are some of the oldest native trees still remaining in the city.

The park and creek were named for the family of Dr. John Bunn, the Red River settlement's first Metis physician. Dr. Bunn was born in 1801 at a company post on Hudson's Bay. He was schooled in Edinburgh and brought back to be the company surgeon at Moose Factory, in 1819. Over time he was employed to travel and give medical care to the entire area of settlement - from York Factory to the Red River Colony. He became a highly popular fellow recognized for extraordinary accomplishments. By 1835, Bunn was not only a physician, but

also the coroner, clerk of the court, and sheriff. He gave much of his time to improving the health and social conditions of the colony and worked in the settlement until he died in 1881.

Kildonan Drive

Start	Fraser's Grove Park on Kildonan Drive
Distance	4.5 km return
Parking	Rossmere Crescent

Walk through groves of elm and ash along the east bank of the Red River. This parkway stretches away from the river like a large village green between Rossmere and Larchdale Crescents. On leaving the pathway, walk down quiet and shady Kildonan Drive to the Bergen cut-off. Climb a path to walk atop the abandoned rail bed that leads to Henderson Highway and a busy shopping and restaurant district.

North Kildonan is part of the oldest settlement in our province. When Kildonan parish was first established by the Selkirk settlers in 1812, farmers occupied river lots on the western side of the river and used the well treed eastern side for fire wood. By 1820, when the west was filled up, people moved across and began to farm on former wood lots.

1 Fraser's Grove Park is named for a second generation Selkirk settler who generously allowed neighbours to picnic on his nicely wooded property. Over the years, Fraser's willingness to extend his hospitality beyond his circle of friends made the area popular as a summer and winter fun spot.

Kildonan
Park

Red River

abandoned rail bed

③

Kildonan Drive

Irving Pl

Henderson Hwy

Fraser's
① Grove Park

Rossmere ②

P

N

Today it's possible to wander through Fraser Grove Park on a summer's night and listen to the music from Rainbow stage in Kildonan Park across the river.

it wound its way across what is now Henderson Highway, Irving Place and Essar Ave. It once even boasted a water mill called Matheson Grist Mill.

2 A beautiful turn-of-the-century house at **135 Rossmere** was originally a river lot farmhouse.

3 Water Mill Creek is now essentially filled-in, but at one time

St Vital

Start	Southwest corner of parking lot
Distance	6 km return
Parking	Parking lot adjacent to duck pond

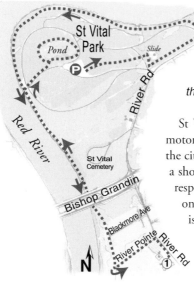

This walk takes you through the thickly wooded landscape of St. Vital Park and along the Red River to the site of a Metis farmhouse wonderfully restored to the era of the early settlers.

St Vital Park was originally designed for motorists. When the land was purchased by the city in 1929, the idea of using a park for a short automobile excursion drew popular response from the citizenry. The emphasis on roadways over walking paths however, is more than compensated by beautiful natural features of the park. Tucked into a bend of the Red River, are sections of thick woods mixed with open meadows and outstanding viewpoints along the high river bank. Wide asphalt pathways border the centrepiece man-made lake and nearby rock garden.

1 Riel House

There are two routes to the Riel farm house, and the river bank route may require some agility, particularly

when wet. The alternative route is down River Road and across busy Bishop Grandin.

The river bank path continues south out of the park, past the cemetery and under Bishop Grandin. Cross Blackmore Avenue to River Point Road; then proceed east to River Road.

This was the home of Louis Riel's family from 1880 to 1969. Riel House is now a National Historic Site. The national importance of Louis Riel is the raison d'etre of Riel House National Historic Park, but its interpretation focuses more specifically on the Riel family and Metis society during the 1860s. The Metis had pursued mixed farming in the parish of St.

Vital since the 1830s, and Riel House displays the typical farm layout. The barn, chicken house, milk house, and

other farm buildings were customarily located close to the river bank for easy access to water and waste disposal. Small fenced and cultivated grain fields were located "at the back", or as in the case of the Riel Farm, in the area between the Red and Seine rivers. Beyond this, occupying the rest of the long narrow lot, was the larger hay field. Cattle were usually allowed to graze in unfenced areas around the barn and probably close to the residence. River Lot 51, occupied by the Riel family in the 1880s, was larger than a standard lot. It was twelve chains (792 feet) in width and two miles in depth, for a total of 232 acres. The property also included a twenty four acre parcel at the Seine River or eastern boundary, where a grist mill was built around 1855.

Since the 1960s, urbanization had been creeping over this originally rural farming district. Since Riel House became an historic park in 1981, a housing development has been built to the west and much of the illusion of a river lot setting as it existed in the 1880s is gone.

Normand Park

Start	Path entrance on Redview Dr
Distance	5 km return
Parking	On Redview Dr

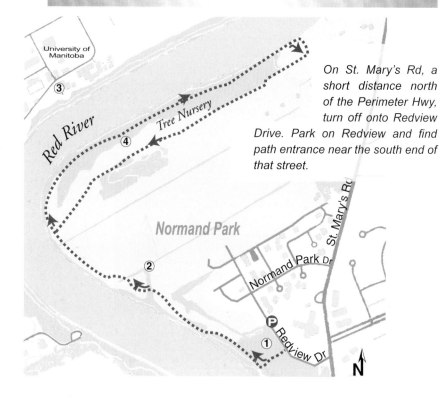

On St. Mary's Rd, a short distance north of the Perimeter Hwy, turn off onto Redview Drive. Park on Redview and find path entrance near the south end of that street.

The first part of this walk is on a carefully landscaped pathway in a new residential development. The second half follows old trails along the river and through the old Henteleff nursery

1 **Normand Park** - This walk begins in an upscale housing development built in 1987 and designed in line with the city's new policy of preserving the river bank for recreation. The Residents' Association and Winnipeg Parks worked together to build a walking path through existing native river forest vegetation with native

grasses and flowers planted in the open areas of this 14 acre linear park.

2 A row of mature willows divide the residential portion of the walk from a dirt trail skirting fields of open meadow. Follow an informal path (that turns into a dirt road) running north and east along the river to the tree nursery.

3 Note the University of Manitoba skyline across the river. Watch for deer and fox in the fields.

4 This **tree nursery**, now operated by the city of Winnipeg, was once the Henteleff family market gardens. They cleared the land in the 1920s and ran their operation until the '60s when the city expropriated the land for a proposed 'Green Zone' around Winnipeg.

| **Start** | Parking lot near sports club |
| **Distance** | 6 km return |

Skirting open fields and winding through mature native river forest, this informal pathway hugs the east bank of the Red River. Even with the Perimeter Hwy often within sight, you have the sense of being in a wild and isolated place.

1 This riverbank forest was once a thriving recreation area called **Maple Grove Beach**. During the forties, swimming, a dance hall, canoe rentals and baseball diamonds beckoned city dwellers to a day of fun 'in the country'. Having reached its peak of popularity as a picnic site during World War II, the facilities were badly damaged in the 1950 flood, and then the beach was declared unsafe for swimming during the polio epidemic of '53.

2 For more than forty years (until the mid '60s), these open fields were home to five market garden operations that employed up to 50 people in a busy summer. They supplied vegetables to Safeway and other grocery stores in the city. In the early thirties, W. A. Taylor, a St. Boniface candy store owner, planted more than 10 acres of horse radish. It was processed on site and sold it under the label 'Poplar'.

The rows of trees that butt up to the riverbank at 1/8 mile intervals are

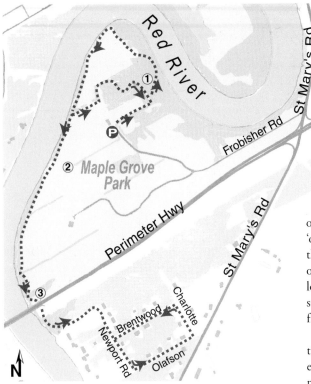

holding pattern on the settlers. This action was one major factor leading to the Metis Resistance of 1869.

In recent history, Maple Grove has gone to the dogs. This is now one of the most popular 'off-leash dog areas' in the city. If you're fond of pooches, you'll love watching them scamper happy and free in the open fields.

The city, at various times, has made elaborate plans for the park's development - fishing piers, a swinging bridge across the river to King's Park, etc., but so far rugby and soccer fields have been the only developments. Nonetheless, the park is a popular all season walk, and hopefully much of it will be preserved in its natural state

evidence of land tenure based on the seigneurial system that was practiced by the early Metis settlers. From the early 1800s, long narrow river lots up to 3 km deep gave families access to water and transportation. Subsequently, the Canadian Government purchased the land from the Hudson's Bay Company and tried to impose the English land

3 **side trip** *Continue on the path under the Perimeter Hwy bridge and through scrub oak woods to Newport Road. Turn left or east on Brentwood, right on Charlotte and right on Olafson to Newport to complete this loop and return.*

Start	John Bruce Rd Foot Bridge
Distance	2.5 km
Parking	John Bruce Rd (East off St Anne's Rd / south of Bishop Grandin)

This walk is a loop comprised of two very different trails along the Seine River. Beginning at John Bruce Road where it crosses the

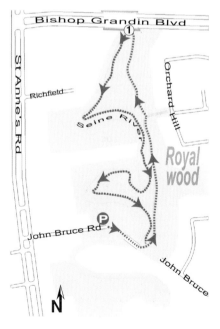

happen upon a deer or a turtle basking in the sun. This river bottom forest has a beautiful mix of poplar, oak and some giant cottonwoods as well as masses of high bush c r a n b e r r y, saskatoon and wild rose. When we walked it in June the trails were white with cranberry blossoms.

Seine, find the foot bridge and take the asphalt path on the east bank that leads to the north. This pathway through open green space skirts the subdivision of Royalwood.

1 Towards its north end the trail winds through a thicket of trees and shrubs and leads down to the river. When you have the Seine River and busy Bishop Grandin Blvd in sight, search for a narrow trail that leads back south. This monkey trail sticks fairly close to the river bank and is very heavily used.

These informal trails are much more interesting than the upper path. Immediately you have a real sense of wilderness. Don't be surprised if you

Construction has begun on an extension of Royalwood Southeast along the Seine River. It will surround an 80 acre pristine forest, 'Bois des Esprit', that has been preserved for a park for passive recreational activities. Developers and the city of Winnipeg plan to extend the Seine River Trail through the forest. Bois-des-esprit was preserved through the efforts of the dedicated members of the Save Our Seine organization who have been stewards of this enchanting river since 1990.

Start	Path to the west of parking area
Distance	2.8 km loop
Parking	Parking Lot - King's Park

Tucked away in Fort Richmond, this riverside park sports one of the best kept walking paths in the city. A wide asphalt trail, meticulously cleared of snow in the winter, follows the banks of the Red through river bottom forest. Along the way you catch a glimpse of open meadows, waterfalls, wild flower gardens and a pond. University of Manitoba students make heavy use of this park, so expect to meet

lots of joggers and cyclists.

The shallow lake complete with a small island and waterfowl nesting area, is the centre piece of the park. In summer, it is often pink with soft-stem bulrushes that can grow eight feet high.

The land excavated from the lake was used to build a hill at its north end and a rockery with three sets of waterfalls. River water is pumped in at the northwest corner of the park and cascades down over the black granite bed of the waterfalls and into the lake. Two bridges connect to the island where a colourful Chinese pagoda, a gift of Winnipeg's Chinese Community, holds centre stage. Native chokecherry, buffalo berry, and jack pine flourish in the rockery, and there are also sea buckthorn, creeping juniper, mugo pine and Nanking cherry. The south end of the park has a trellised sitting area from which you can view the arboretum and native wildflower and prairie grasses garden.

King's Park was unique during the 1997 spring flood in that it was one of the few civic green spaces to be purposely flooded in order to save the surrounding neighbourhood. A dike was constructed just inside the north border of the park by heavy construction equipment which removed earth and clay from the bermed area near the waterfall. After all usable clay was removed from the park, clean fill was trucked in. This resulted in a protective dike that was wider than 20 feet at the base and over 12 feet tall near the river. When the flood waters reached their peak, King's Park was flooded flush with the main entrance gate off King's Drive. It appeared as if the river had swallowed the park whole, with water depths ranging from one to over fifteen feet.

It took a long time for the park to recover. Much replanting needed to be done. The new dike was landscaped and incorporated into the park, and the pit where clay was "borrowed" was developed into a feature. These changes serve as a reminder of the great power of the Red River to reshape its surroundings.

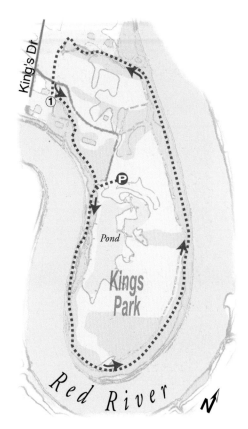

The neighbourhood around King's Park wasn't developed until 1945. One of its best known residents was Dr. E.J. Washington, who owned a good deal of property in the area. In fact the King's Park land was once called Washington Peninsula. There is a story fondly remembered, that when the doctor allowed a portion of this land to be worked by a market gardener, he insisted that a beautiful old elm tree be left unharmed.

1 That elm stands to this day, just a few feet off King's Drive on the right hand side of the park entrance roadway and is recognized as a heritage tree.

Crescent Drive

Start	Crescent Drive Park Picnic Shelter
Distance	3.2 km loop
Parking	Parking Lot - Crescent Drive Park

This route takes woodland paths through the riverside city park and quiet neighbourhood of Crescent Park.

Walk towards the river from the parking lot; then follow the dike path north past the boat launch to Crane Avenue; turn up Crane and follow it past Buxton Road, then turn right off Crane onto a footpath between Buxton Road and Sandra Bay.

This is a lovely walk for a family outing. The route through the park hugs a mile of river bank under tall shady trees, then meanders through the community of Crescent Park where many homes border on well treed green space. The circular route ends at a very pleasant picnic site and playground.

Crescent Park was an unoccupied rural municipality of woods and unbroken prairie as late as 1920s. Going back for centuries, this would have been prime sugar bush. Groves of Manitoba maple thrived in this crescent of rich alluvial soil and their syrup provided an important source of food for early settlers.

The spring sugar making season was always a happy time, marking as it did the close of a hard prairie winter. Toward the end of March, when it was warm during the day but freezing at night, whole families would make their annual trip to the sugar camps. There was work for each member of the family. The men tapped the trees by cutting long slanting gashes in the trunk and driving in flat grooved wedges of wood. From these spigots, the sap, pale and colourless as water, dripped into pails hung below. Women and children gathered the sap

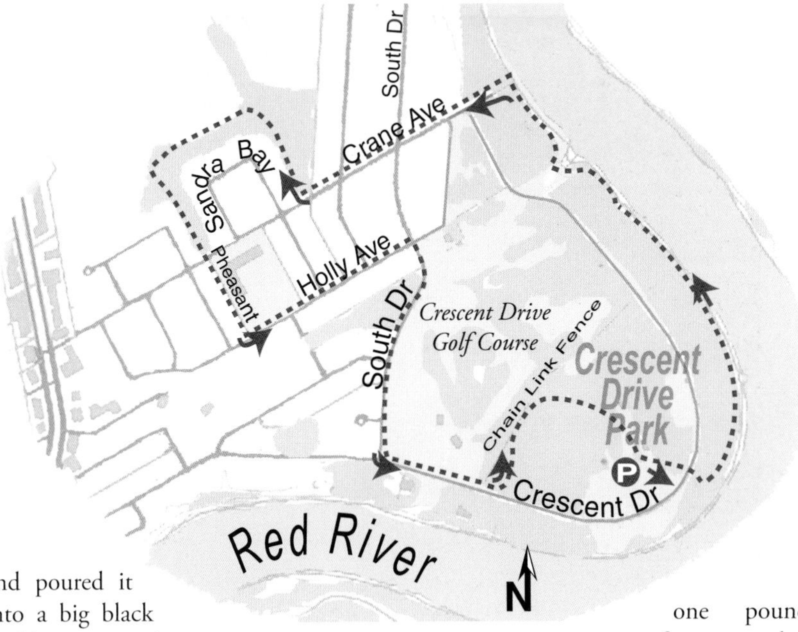
South Dr
Crane Ave
Sandra Bay
Pheasant
Holly Ave
South Dr
Crescent Drive
Golf Course
Chain Link Fence
Crescent
Drive
Park
P
Crescent Dr
Red River
N

and poured it into a big black cauldron over a hot fire. When boiled down sufficiently, it was poured into shallow dishes and left to harden, after which it was turned out in the form of a solid cake. Ordinarily it took 40 gallons of sap to produce one pound of sugar and a small camp might produce 25-30 lb. of sugar a season. Maple sugar was of particular importance to early settlers as it was used as an item of trade.

Wildwood

Start	Wildwood St at Manchester Blvd
Distance	3.6 km loop
Parking	Manchester Blvd

This circle route winds through the woodsy neighbourhood of Wildwood Park and down a country lane that intersects the Wildewood Golf Course. Off season, you are welcome to walk across the golf course greens and along the Red River dike.

Begin on the pedestrian walkway that runs east and then south through the neighbourhood's central strip of parkland.

In 1946, Wildwood Park was the first residential 'garden suburb' on the Prairies. The development was intended to meet the housing shortage after World War II, and the basic design was based on a highly celebrated development in Radburn, New Jersey. It's interesting that what began as a low cost housing experiment has turned into some very pricey and desirable real estate. Wildwood Park remains today the most unique housing development in the city.

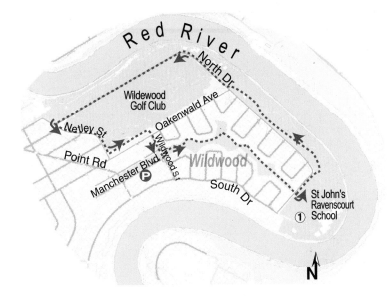

All the homes in this 87 acre development face onto greenspace that is heavily treed and laced with pedestrian walkways. There are no streets running through the neighbourhood, just service lanes circling its periphery and behind the houses. The lanes form ten residential bays, identified alphabetically from A through J. Wildwood originally contained 281 houses with only five different floor plans available. The development proved so popular over the years, that most of these modest cottages have been transformed beyond recognition.

The park is filled with mature elms, ash and oak trees. Gardens are creatively landscaped. As you walk through the park there are many paths running east and west that you may wish to explore.

1 Once through the park and out on to South Drive, **St. John's Ravenscourt** School is to your right. Through the trees of the Ravenscourt grounds, you can glimpse the rooftop of a Victorian mansion with a sad and romantic past. Colonel R.M. Thompson hired architect Cyril Chivers to design this house and had it built for his new bride. Before they could move in, he was called away to serve in World War I, where he died in battle. His distraught young widow refused to move into the house after that, and it remained empty for almost 20 years. With its aura of mystery, the mansion soon became a mini tourist attraction, and its private lane made a popular Sunday drive for Winnipeggers. The house is now used as a residence for St. John's Ravenscourt students.

Churchill Parkway - North Section

Start	The Forks
Turn Around	Riverview Community Gardens
Distance	8 km return

Our map shows the route of the Churchill Parkway along the west bank of the Red River all the way from the Norwood Bridge down a long narrow strip of green space called Churchill Drive Park to Cockburn Street. Because of its length, we've broken it up into two hikes - one beginning at The Forks and one at the Elm Park foot bridge. We've also included two loops through the attractive neighbourhoods of Kingston Crescent and Riverview. The community gardens behind the Riverview Health Centre serve as the end point or turn-around

Churchill Parkway - South Section

Start	Elm Park foot bridge
Turn Around	Riverview Community Gardens
Distance	8 km return
Parking	Kingston Crescent

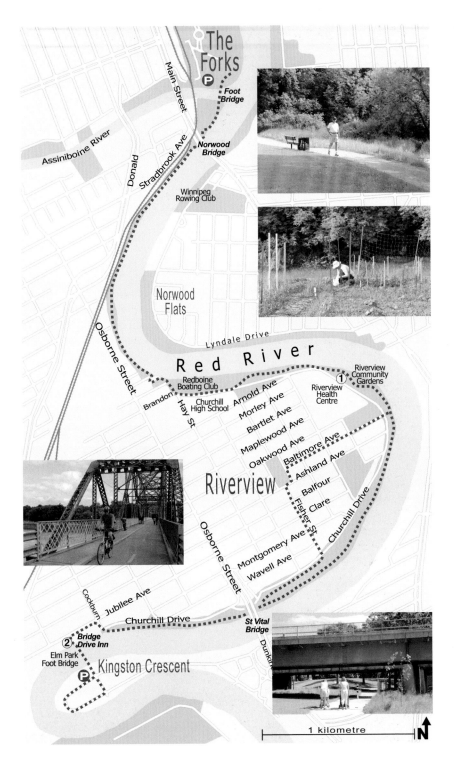

The Forks

Foot Bridge

Main Street

Norwood Bridge

Assiniboine River

Donald

Stradbrook Ave

Winnipeg Rowing Club

Norwood Flats

Osborne Street

Lyndale Drive

Red River

Redboine Boating Club

Brandon

Hay St

Churchill High School

Arnold Ave

Morley Ave

Bartlet Ave

Maplewood Ave

Oakwood Ave

Baltimore Ave

Ashland Ave

Balfour

Fisher St

Clare

Riverview Health Centre

Riverview Community Gardens

①

Churchill Drive

Riverview

Osborne Street

Montgomery Ave

Wavell Ave

Cockburn

Jubilee Ave

Churchill Drive

St Vital Bridge

Dunkirk

② Bridge Drive Inn

Elm Park Foot Bridge

Kingston Crescent

1 kilometre

N

point for both walks.

1 **Riverview Community Gardens** - This fertile land has a long history of producing a bounty of vegetables. For years the adjacent municipal hospitals had huge gardens and greenhouses here and brought in inmates from Headingley

penitentiary every day to plant and weed. In the 1970s the hospitals were sold to the province and the gardens leased to the Riverview Community Garden society. This is some of the richest soil in the city. Be sure to check out the crops!

Until the second World War, most of the Riverview area was taken up with the River Park carnival and exhibition grounds. For Winnipeggers this was the just the place for a day's outing. The privately owned River Park had a great assortment of attractions including a zoo with lions and tigers, a miniature train, and a roller coaster. Going back even earlier to the 1890s, you read about pleasure seekers riding a ferry across the Red River to the Elm Park fair grounds or Kingston Crescent

as it is now called. Here the many amusements included a hike through an enchanted forest. It was obviously an enlightened age because by all reports the walk through towering elms was every bit as popular as any other carnival attraction.

2 The **Bridge Drive Inn** or BDI as it's commonly know, is a Winnipeg institution and most summer days will see it packed with loyal customers. Nearby the picturesque old Elm Park bridge, now open to foot traffic only, beckons you to cross the river to beautiful tree-lined Kingston Crescent.

Start	Kingsway Ave
Distance	5.5 km loop
Parking	Kingsway at Wellington Crescent

This route through one of our older neighbourhoods shows off some of the most imposing homes in the city. It includes a stroll down the trendy Corydon strip and ends at Munson Park on the Assiniboine River.

Crescentwood was largely undeveloped until 1895 when a bridge was built over the Assiniboine at the site of the present Maryland Bridge. This coincided with the deterioration of the city's most affluent district near the present Fort Garry Hotel. In the days before zoning, conflicting land uses meant that a brewery might be built next door to a mansion. It was time to move!

Developer C. H. Enderton saw his opportunity and he was determined to make his new 'subdivision' of Crescentwood the most sought after address in the city. A caveat was placed on each lot, requiring the dwelling to be set back 60 feet from the front street line and have a value of at least $3500.00 - a tidy sum in those days. On Wellington Crescent the minimum figure was $6000. These restrictions ensured that single-family

residential use would predominate, and Crescentwood has been a popular haven for the 'economically advantaged' ever since. Although there was a weakening of restrictions during the depression and World Wars, the spirit of the community was restored in 1952 when the Crescentwood Home Owners Association emerged and actively devoted themselves to maintaining the Enderton legacy of the single family neighbourhood.

Crescentwood contains some of the most impressive early 20th century homes in Winnipeg, if not in western Canada. A detailed historical walking tour of Crescentwood is available from the Manitoba Historical Society.

2 Once past **Munson Park**'s tyndall stone pillars and wrought iron fencing, you'll find woodlands that have been preserved in much of their original state. A.E. Munson, a Winnipeg lawyer, built Crescentwood Home here in the late 1880s. He retained the natural landscaping which was quite rare within the city at this time. In 1919, James Richardson purchased the property. His family lived here for 57 years until 1973, when they donated it to the city as a park. A plaque reads - "the existing trail through prairie scrub extending along the fence was originally created by natives and early pioneers, travelling from Upper Fort Garry to the West".

1 **Corydon Avenue** between Pembina and Stafford has a Mediterranean flavour with its cappuccino bars, Florentine light standards, and a fine assortment of restaurants. Nicknamed "Little Italy", this is one of the trendiest dining and shopping areas in the city.

Start	Omand's Park
Distance	5.5 km loop
Parking	On Raglan Rd

This route crosses the Assiniboine River twice and takes you through two very different neighbourhoods. Wellington Crescent has the highest concentration of grand mansions in the city and a lovely boulevard pathway. The Wolseley area is generally viewed as Winnipeg's 'granola belt'. In the last decade, many young families have moved to the area, attracted by its strong sense of community, Laura Secord School, and handsome older houses.

1 Entering Omand's Park off Raglan Road, take note of 1339 Wolseley Avenue (**Pioneer Lodge**), which was built by Frederick Salter around 1880. A skilled gardener, Salter owned the two lots east of Omands Creek and kept 26 greenhouses which supplied the C.P.R. trains from Montreal to Vancouver. Raglan Road was originally his private lane until the Wolseley area was subdivided in 1910.

3 Not that long ago, **Wellington Crescent** was just an Indian trail following the curves of the river. There was no settlement until the mid 1880s, and locals referred to this part of town as 'the Bush'. In 1893 it was named for lawyer Arthur Wellington Ross who had purchased land in the area.

4 1015 Wellington Crescent (often referred to as the **Eaton mansion**) was designed by Arther Cubbidge in the mock Tudor style. Cubbidge was a British architect responsible for a number of massive houses in the city.

5 On Wolseley Avenue between Chestnut and Canora, there are four distinctive brick houses on riverlot properties. The corner house (**838 Wolseley**) is one of only a handful of residences to have heritage building designation. Its back porches are particularly impressive and were built to signify the status of the owner to his Wellington Crescent neighbours across the river.

6 A mass of colourful blooms greet you as you turn up **Ethelbert** Street. Many streets in the city now have beautiful boulevard and front yard

Note: *During the summer months on Sundays and holidays, Wellington Crescent and Wolseley are limited to pedestrians and cyclists.*

flower gardens, but Ethelbert was one of the first and still one of the best.

2 *side trip* Instead of crossing the river at the railway foot bridge, continue west across the rail tracks on a well maintained path that follows the river behind the old church yard to Wolseley West. Here you'll find St. James Anglican Church, the oldest wooden church left standing in western Canada. It was completed in 1853 at a cost of $1620 and still has services during summer months. **Note: Restaurants and the Polo Park shopping mall are just one short block north up Tylehurst.**

7 As you turn onto **Westminster** Avenue, you enter the area's 'counter culture' business strip consisting of shops, eateries, and one of the city's most popular bakeries. Turn left or south on Ruby Street and head back down to Palmerston.

8 Laura Secord School (960 Wolseley) stands at the very heart

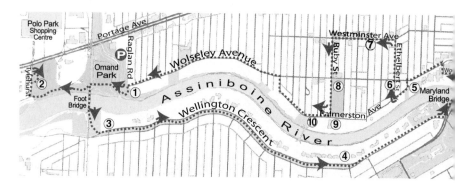

9 As evidenced by a proliferation of beautiful flowers on Wolseley boulevards, gardening is a passion for many local residents. **Robert A. Steen Community Club** (980 Palmerston) is home to the Wolseley Garden Society, which organizes popular garden tours every summer. In front of the club, an elm tree has been planted to commemorate one of the city's most spectacular acts of civil disobedience. In 1957, twelve otherwise law abiding ladies defied city hall and won the right to save a landmark 100 year old elm tree from the ax.

of the neighbourhood. The architectural detail of the school was lovingly restored in 1980s, and the building stands as a symbol for the refurbishment taking place in many of the older homes in the neighbourhood.

10 **1006 Palmerston** is part of an original farm house built in the early 1870s (probably the oldest home in the area). The river farm lot originally extended two miles north across Portage to Notre Dame Avenue.

Start	Assiniboine Park Footbridge
Distance	7 km return
Parking	Parking lot by Duck Pond

Walking through this quiet neighbourhood of well kept homes and enormous gardens, you'll discover the wealth of green space these St. James residents enjoy.

From the duck pond, walk through the north edge of Assiniboine Park to a landmark footbridge on the Assiniboine River; cross over and then head east.

Bruce Park is named for two pioneer farmers who settled in this area. Today we can still enjoy the lilac bushes that James Bruce, an avid gardener, planted near what is now the west end of Deer Lodge Place.

1 A bronze plaque commemorates celebrated resident **LeMoine Fitzgerald** (a member of Canada's famous "Group of Seven"), who lived at #30 Deer Lodge Place. Fitzgerald's painting of "Doc Snyders House" hangs in the National Gallery. Other works can be seen at the St. James Library and Winnipeg Art Gallery.

2 This 13 acre park on the banks of **Truro Creek** is a showpiece with ancient trees, plantings of blue spruce and clump birch, wild roses, an ornamental footbridge, and rolling landscape.

3 *Follow paths through Bruce Park, cross creek bridge and exit on back lane near north end of park. Proceed down lane to library; then turn right and follow informal path along back* **gardens of Douglas Park Road** *. You'll be rewarded with a terrific view of the massive lots and beautiful gardens on this street.*

4 A walk by the Bourkevale Community Club in the right season may offer you a glimpse of the stately game of **lawn bowling**. The club has an active contingent of bowlers who put on a fine show on many a summer afternoon.

5 Bourkevale Avenue is named for **John Bourke**, one of the earliest farmers in the area and a celebrated buffalo hunter. Bourke was one of the many men who came out from the British Isles to work in the fur trade for the Hudson's Bay Co. Like many of his co-workers, he fell in love with the place and decided to settle down on this part of the Assiniboine River.

6 A number of interesting **shops and eateries** have sprung up on Portage Ave across from the park footbridge. A coffee house, ice cream parlour and an antique and used book store provide an attractive destination for this walk.

Old Tuxedo

Start	Assiniboine Park Conservatory
Distance	4 km loop
Parking	Conservatory Parking Lot

This is an attractive walk that takes in woodlands paths, formal flower gardens, a world famous sculpture garden, and a sidewalk tour of the stately homes of Old Tuxedo. The loop begins and ends at the Assiniboine Park Conservatory.

Assiniboine Park is what most of us grew up thinking of as a proper park - expansive lawns, wooded picnic sites, playgrounds, paved paths and plenty of trees. A zoo, conservatory, sculpture garden, and Tudor style pavilion complete the picture. As Winnipeg's largest park (393 acres), this is often referred to as 'City Park'.

The plan for Assiniboine Park, created in 1904, was based on the design of Frederick Law Olmsted - the father of landscape architecture in North America. The style is one that was used commonly throughout North America around the turn of the century and features curvilinear roadways, geometrical flower gardens, free form or serpentine ponds, and open meadows and lawns backed by borders of native plants. The curving paths and roadways were meant to provide relief from the grid pattern of urban streets.

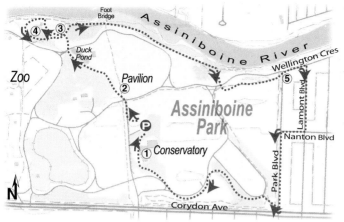

4 Adjacent to the English gardens is the **Leo Mol Sculpture Garden**. Mol is a Winnipeg artist whose naturalistic sculptures are internationally renowned.

1 The **Conservatory** provides plant lovers with a lush year round oasis. It features a Palm house with tropical trees and exotic plants, and a continuous display of flowering and foliage plants in a garden setting.

2 The **Pavilion** was designed to suggest the English countryside and has been a city landmark for nearly 100 years. Its refurbished interior now houses an art centre and an elegant glass enclosed restaurant.

3 In summer, the **English Garden** is an explosion of colour with its formal flower beds of annuals and roses, and a lily pond surrounded by shade trees. At its east entrance, amidst the pool plantings is the 'Boy with the Boot' fountain statue. This statue is special to Winnipeggers. It was given to the city in 1897 by the Young People's Christian Endeavour Society and it used to stand in front of city hall. Then it disappeared and was listed as missing for 30 years. Mysteriously, it showed up by the duck pond in Assiniboine Park one day in the 1940s. The people at city hall were mystified but decided to install it right where it had been found.

5 In 1913, the Town of **Tuxedo** was planned by a small group of men, as an exclusive and secluded development. To forestall any possibility of low or even medium-priced housing being built, a minimum value of $10,000 was imposed for each proposed dwelling. As well, each house had to be a minimum of 15 metres back from the street and each lot needed to measure at least 23 by 40 metres. These tight building regulations essentially dictated that each house have the look of a country estate, and in fact, many were patterned after grand Tudor or Georgian style English manor houses.

Assiniboine Forest

Start	Parking Lot at Grant and Chalfont
Distance	5 km return

Assiniboine Forest is the largest urban forest park in Canada. It was established as a centennial project in 1974 and with the exception of the pond area, is maintained in its natural state.

Nowhere else within the boundaries of the city will a walker feel as surrounded by nature on this massive scale. This is a true urban wilderness.

1 Eve Werier Pond - The pond (named after Werier who devoted much of her time to wildlife preservation) is a man-made ecosystem constructed by Ducks Unlimited in the late 1970s. It supplies water for wild life and waterfowl, and with this water source, deer can be saved from crossing busy streets to reach the Assiniboine River. As well, the marsh is home to myriad wetland species - cattails, bulrushes and duckweed are most abundant. Early

mornings or at dusk you may come upon deer drinking at water's edge or see a flock of ducks feeding on wetland plants.

Once you've left the asphalt path, heading south, you enter an aspen / oak forest consisting mainly of trembling aspen interspersed with oak. Underbrush includes dogwood, hazelnut, saskatoon, and chokecherry. This habitat is home to the white-tailed deer, the red squirrel, and the great horned owl.

Running off the main trail at regular intervals are a number of paths which are very wet in spring. These paths are the road cuts made in 1920 in readiness for a housing development which fortunately never happened.

The route passes through many small prairie clearings that indicate a meadow ecosystem. These clearings contain a

plant community very different from that in the aspen / oak forest and most of these prairie plant and animal species are becoming quite rare. Species include big bluestem grass, yellow lady slipper, bird foot violets and meadow blazingstar. Watch for kingbirds and meadowlarks.

2 At the south end of the park, our path abuts a footpath called the **Harte Trail**. This path runs west on an abandoned rail line to the perimeter highway and beyond. If you are interested in a long distance trek, you can follow it all the way to Beaudry Park.

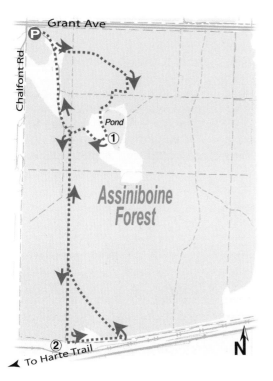

Harte Trail

Start	Ridgewood Avenue & Haney Street
Distance	9 km return
Parking	Haney Street

This former railway line is a 12 mile linear parkway running east / west from the south edge of Assiniboine Forest, through Charleswood, across the Perimeter Highway and past Headingley to Beaudry Park.

Our walk picks up the trail at its most attractive point at Haney Street and Ridgewood Avenue in Charleswood.

Over the years fruit bearing shrubs, Siberian elm and other native plants have grown up as shelter. This is a perfect local example of how a variety of natural growth takes over when land is left alone. The trail is regularly used for cycling and cross country skiing, as well

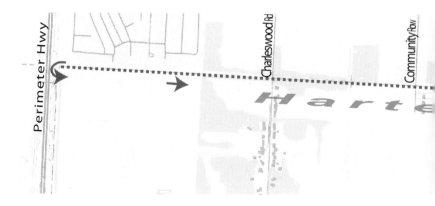

as walking. Expect to share with dog walkers and cyclists.

The Harte Line was the first section built by the Grand Trunk Pacific Railway in western Canada and was in use from 1894 to 1972. It takes its name from a community further down the line, that no longer exists.

Along the path, a grove of spruce and another of cottonwood mark former farmsteads.

The path is intersected by half a dozen streets, and it is clear where the locals gain access, from numerous well worn footpaths meeting the trail. Housing developers continue to eye the land in this corridor, but Charleswood residents are wisely protecting their wilderness strip.

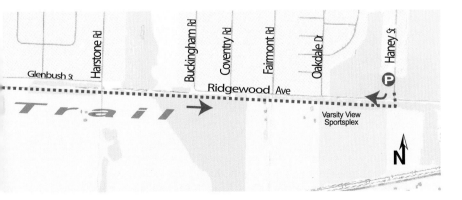

Southboine

Start	Footbridge in Beauchemin Park
Distance	5.5 km return
Parking	Elmvale Cres

Although this is a trek through suburbia, it's filled with historical significance.

From Elmvale Crescent, take the path across the Beaverdam Creek footbridge, through Beauchemin Park and out along Southboine Drive.

Beauchemin Park is named for Baptiste Beauchemin, one of the many Metis who were employed in the fur trade and later settled in Charleswood in the 1860s.

1 'The Passage' at the end of Berkley Ave is the site of an ancient ford on the Assiniboine and a designated cultural landmark. Shallow waters made this a choice location for bison herds to cross, and during the fur trade era, Native hunters guided the European traders to this ford.

Cuthbert Grant and his followers crossed here in 1816, trying to avoid the confrontation that resulted in the Battle of Seven Oaks, and Lord Selkirk's troops met Chief Peguis at The Passage in 1817 before recapturing Fort Douglas.

2 A path running north off Southboine between #6343 and #6363, leads to a greenspace named **Kelly's Landing**. A store called Kelly's Landing was established near The Passage to capitalize on the flow of traffic. Today the Kelly's Landing site and the river bank property between it and Beauchemin Park are owned by the City of Winnipeg, which hopefully will develop and incorporate it into the City Park system.

Follow Southboine west; cross a playground called Daly Gardens; then follow Barker Blvd to Musgrove St which takes you to the entrance of Caron Park.

3 **Caron Park** has wide open meadows, dirt paths and bluffs of

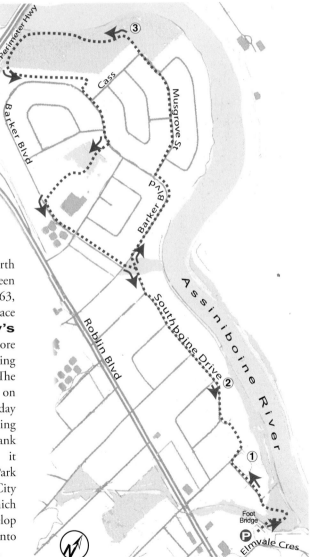

trees near the river that fit with the informal nature of this park. It is part of what was once four-mile strips of farmland running back from the Assiniboine to what is still called Four Mile Road, south of Wilkes Avenue. The first settlers were the Caron brothers in the 1880s, and the Caron farmhouse at the Musgrove entrance is the only original farmhouse left on the Assiniboine River. It gives a sense of this neighbourhood before the turn of the century.

The Carons built the first ferry to take their cheese across the Assiniboine to the Portage Trail. In winter they would walk across the river ice to church. During spring break-up they needed to go all the way down to the Polo Park area to cross the river, which meant an hour and a half journey to church each Sunday.

Exit park and turn left on Barker Blvd. Follow that street until you reach LaFleche Park. Cross the park and school grounds to regain Barker Blvd where you turn left. Follow Barker back to cross Dale Blvd and Southboine Drive back to your starting point.

Start	Walking bridge at end of Woodbridge Rd
Distance	9 km return
Parking	Woodbridge Road

This is a long gentle walk that winds through the pretty neighbourhood of Woodhaven then follows the narrow parkway that borders Sturgeon Creek from the Assiniboine River all the way to Saskatchewan Avenue.

Begin the walk near the junction of Sturgeon Creek and the Assiniboine River at Ashcroft Point - a favorite fishing spot with the locals. A walking bridge over Sturgeon Creek leads to the community of Woodhaven and Woodhaven Park.

Woodhaven is a picturesque neighbourhood bounded by the Assiniboine River, Sturgeon Creek and the St Charles Country Club on the west. Residents enjoy a particularly fine vista of the broad Sturgeon Creek valley. The first houses built in this area were summer homes, and the community has retained the air of a quieter and more relaxed time. There are no sidewalks and the older narrow roads wind and dip with the terrain.

1 St Charles Country Club sets the standard for prestige. How many golf clubs can boast they've been played by the Prince of Wales? When first established in 1904, the club was so careful of its reputation that when the head of the household applied for membership, the entire family was screened. The price of membership was another challenge, with entrance fees at $100 on top of a $100 debenture and yearly membership at $25 for gentlemen, $10 for ladies, and $5 for clergymen.

Exit Woodhaven on an asphalt path under Portage Avenue which brings you out near Grant's Mill.

Grant's Mill is named for Cuthbert Grant who is best remembered as the leader of the Metis at the battle of Seven Oaks. Son of a Scottish father and a Cree mother, Grant was born in 1793 at a North West Company trading post where his father was the factor. He was sent to Scotland for his education and returned to work for the Northwest Company.

This is a replica of a mill constructed by Grant in the 1830s. It was the first of its kind to be built in the west. The mill was used for grinding flour and featured a huge water wheel. But Grant's enterprise encountered endless problems. The 230 foot dam that he constructed collapsed repeatedly, and eventually he was flooded out entirely

and moved his operation to Grantown (now called St. Francis Xavier) and used a wind-driven mill.

From the mill, the path runs parallel to gently sloping grassy banks of the creek. While sections of the bank have been allowed to sprout some natural growth and a few areas have been planted to shrubs and perennials, for the most part, the parkway is open hay meadow. A change to allowing a more naturalized growth is apparent. Bridges and paths lead to the suburban neighbourhoods of Crestview, Heritage Park and Sturgeon Creek. At Ness and Hamilton it is necessary to cross in traffic. By the time you reach Saskatchewan Avenue, open prairie is in view. This walk is best done in spring or fall, or early morning, as there is little shade from the sun on a hot summer day.

This parkway was almost lost to development in the 1970s. Then, new municipal legislation was passed that required developers to set aside adequate space for parks and recreation and also preserve the natural features of the landscape when planning a new development. But legislation is often not enough when valuable land is at stake and in spite of the new agreement, the city was tempted to sell the land. Happily the citizens' cry could be heard - "Come hell or high water you can't have our creek" and their crusade saved the parkway from bulldozers.

2 **Grant's Mill** - *A working replica of Grant's Mill was constructed in 1973 by an enterprising group of St. James-Assiniboia senior citizens. The mill is built from logs cut with a broad axe and held together with nails and wooden pegs. Over the years, the mill has survived the floods and become quite a tourist attraction .*

Start	Parking lot on Farmers Road
Distance	2 km loop

Little Mountain Park is a height of land on a limestone ridge. Our route runs through 80 acres of heavy woodland and around an old quarry. From a rock outcropping at the south end of the park, the whole skyline of Winnipeg is clearly visible ten miles in the distance.

This park has an interesting history. More than 100 years ago, it was home to a village named Mount Royal and a stone crushing operation which was the first limestone quarry of the city of Winnipeg. At peak production, 164 families lived here and worked in the quarry. The village had two blacksmiths, a pool hall, and even a bootlegger. But by 1905 it became too costly to mine in this location. The crusher was dismantled and moved by horse-drawn sled to the present day quarry at Stony Mountain.

Little Mountain is a natural park with a large section of aspen forest. Bur oak, saskatoon, wild plum and chokecherry, as well as dogbane and raspberry, make a dense undergrowth in this edge environment which is home to the red fox.

Our path takes you through authentic prairie. Crocuses can be seen almost as soon as the snow melts and are succeeded by a continuous bloom of wildflowers throughout the summer.

Three flowered Avens, Puccoon, Gallardia and Prairie lilies are some of the blossoms that flourish in this grass parkland.

1 This beautifully shaped Cottonwood is the last remaining planted tree of the lost village of Mount Royal.

2 One of the nicest features of this park

is the old quarry pits - now a scenic pond and picnic site. Paths take you down to the waters edge where jagged limestone walls tower above you. This is a watering hole for all sorts of animals and migratory birds and supports a growth of true water plants.

Beaudry Park

Start	Beaudry Park west of Headingley & north off PR241
Distance	7 km loop

These lovely paths wind under a canopy of towering trees. Beaudry is a natural park with a rare hardwood forest older than the city. The park is home to some of the largest cottonwoods in the province (14 feet in circumference), as well as some 200 year old oaks, American elms that have survived Dutch Elm disease, large and magnificent willows, Manitoba maple and basswood, which are at the northern limit of their range. These trees are river bottom forest, so called because of periodic flooding of the encircling Assiniboine.

Wild grapes scale some of the trees to a height of 15 metres, growing on vines as thick as your arm. There is a diversity of terrain and a diversity of wildlife in the park. Some 95 species of song birds, as well as rabbits, squirrels, beaver, porcupine, coyotes, bears, wildcats, deer, elk and moose can be found.

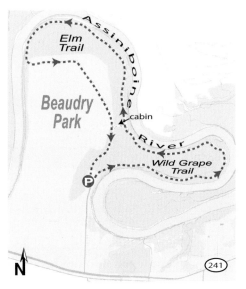

Start   East end of town of Birds Hill on PR 202
Distance   3 km loop

This trail is worth hiking just to witness how wonderfully nature can heal itself with a little help. For a hundred years this was a great gaping hole in the earth, source of 'Birds Hill Gold', the name they gave to a seemingly endless supply of gravel and stone.

The quarry was reborn as Silver Springs Park in 1992. It was the brainchild of the Swistuns, a local family prominent in the gravel industry. Their hard work on this site was the largest industrial rehabilitation project in Manitoba and has added a precious resource to the town of Birds Hill.

Start   St Norbert Community Centre 3450 Pembina Hwy
Distance   5.5 km return

St Norbert volunteers have produced an outstanding walking guide to their heritage trails complete with colourful local history, photographs, and maps. It's available at the community centre and is well worth picking up.

Our route takes in just a portion of the trails in that guide. We begin at the community centre / farmers market on Pembina Hwy and then head east along the dike foot trail that borders the beautiful grounds of Villa Maria Retreat Centre.

1 If you've never been to the St Norbert Farmers Market, you're in for a treat. Every Saturday from June to Thanksgiving, hundreds of vendors from all over the province hawk everything from potatoes to patio furniture and make this the largest outdoor market in Manitoba.

2 As you walk east and south along the dike foot path, you skirt Villa Maria Retreat Centre, a facility established by the Oblate Order of Catholic priests

in 1960. Today followers from many beliefs come here from all over the world to seek relief from the stress of daily life. This secluded setting is criss-crossed by a series of intersecting trails and liberally studded with striking statues and unique shelters built of fieldstone.

3 At the end of rue St Pierre, you'll come to a private lane that hasn't been accessible by car since the 1997 flood. Despite the many No Trespassing signs, it's clear that many people walk in and explore this incredible property. The narrow lane is bounded by the Red River to the east and the LaSalle to the west and offers an interesting view of the floodway gates.

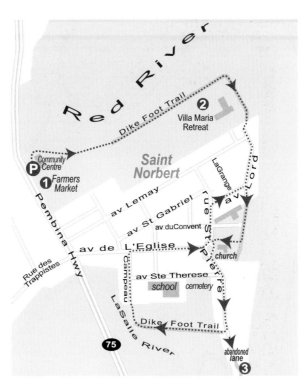

La Barrier Park

Start   Parking Lot - LaBarriere Park
Distance   West Trail 2.6 km / East Trail 4.8 km

Waverley Street leads directly to La Barrier Park which is 3/4 of a mile south of the perimeter highway. There's a sharp dip in the road before the park entrance at the LaSalle River bed. It's also marked by a dam across the river, where you can spot fishermen trying their luck.

These are riverbank trails through acres of lowland forest on the banks of the LaSalle. The park is named for the barrier erected by Louis Riel's followers in 1869. Their act effectively prevented the entry of arms and an unauthorized governor, sent by Ottawa, into the Red River settlement. It was a watershed event in the Metis battle for self-government and a cross standing in St Norbert marks the historic site.

LaBarrier Park offers an enormous riverbank trail system on the river's wooded banks. The lowland forest rolls gently on either side with graceful groves of ash, elm and large stands of

oak. Some of the land consists of original farm river lots, with the woods preserved intact.

This linear river parkway is preserving a unique landscape. The southwest corner of the park is left untended to illustrate the natural state of river forest. The park is also a site for testing the effectiveness of reseeding of native vegetation.

Picnic areas have been mostly cleared of underbrush and given an open and natural setting. The scrub oak trees that dot the upper area are gradually being replaced with elm and ash. Although the city has done some landscaping it is always with the idea of keeping this area a natural beauty spot.

Residents of St. Norbert have drawn up long-range plans for the city to acquire sufficient riverbank access so that a trail eight kilometres long would link La Barrier to the St. Norbert Heritage Park on the Red River.

West trail -

Cross rolling lawns to a foot bridge across the LaSalle. A circle route leads through riverbank woods and up

along the edge of cultivated fields.

East trail - Follow a rough and uneven path along the winding river and return by heading south through a grassy area used by the Boy Scouts' Camp Amisk.

Start	Parking Area for each trail
Distance	Cedar Bog Trail 3.5 km loop
	Whitetail Trail 1.5 km loop

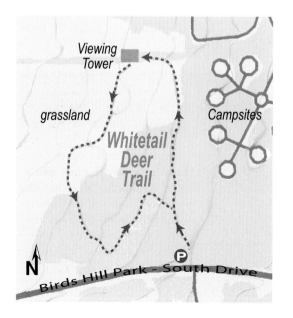

We've chosen two hikes in Bird's Hill Park that are excellent for winter walking. They're both fairly sheltered and nicely snow-packed.

Parts of Birds Hill have an elevation as much as 150 feet above that in Winnipeg. In the great floods of 1826 and 1852, settlers and wildlife found refuge here. Families camped for weeks with their livestock and all the

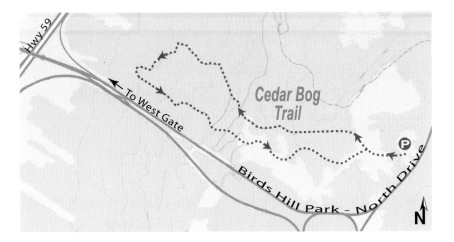

Cedar Bog Trail

To West Gate

Hwy 59

Birds Hill Park - North Drive

N

possessions they could carry.

The unique Birds Hill landscape is really a series of eskers or massive sand and gravel deposits left behind by melted glaciers. As well, the land was sculpted by Lake Agassiz as it drained. Boulders were dropped by melting icebergs 10,000 years ago and as the lake level lowered, Birds Hill became an island. Whenever the lake's level remained constant for several decades, gravelly beaches were formed on the island's shore. Today, these beach ridges are evident along the Cedar Bog Trail

The Cedar Bog Trail winds through stands of aspen and oak interspersed with patches of lush grassland before it descends gently into a unique cedar bog. Here the tall white cedars create a canopy which blocks sunlight and creates mysterious shadows. In winter, brilliant yellow evening grosbeak, black capped chickadees and redpols frequent bird feeders set along the trail.

The White-tailed Deer Trail meanders through aspen groves and across large meadows. This is the place to see deer in their natural habitat. Early in the day you may spot a white tailed deer feeding along the edge of a clearing. If alarmed, the deer will snort and bound away with white tail raised and waving side to side, warning other deer of your presence. A viewing tower is located midway along the trail.

Seine River

Start	Riverbank behind St Boniface Golf Club
Distance	6 km return
Parking	Club Parking Lot at 100 Youville

The largest section of this route is on the ice covered Seine River which has a sheltered well-trodden path in winter. The return route is through the quiet neighbourhood of Glenwood.

Our route begins at the club house of the privately owned St. Boniface Country Club whose members generously allow walkers access to the river in the winter. Walk down to the river bed and proceed south or to the right. The Seine River takes the typical meandering course of most rivers on the flat prairie, and its frozen bed offers a unique place to walk mid winter. When the sun is shining, the light slanting through branches on the well treed banks creates an exquisite scene. On the west bank is the neighbourhood of Glenwood with some of the nicest back yards in Winnipeg. The locals make heavy use of the river as a pathway and for skating and skiing.

For many years the Seine was used as

a garbage dump and its potential ignored, but in 1990 a group of concerned citizens formed the Save Our Seine (S.O.S.). The organization was born out of concern for the plight of this river which flowed past many of their back yards. The group got together volunteer cleanup crews every Thanksgiving and hauled barge loads of shopping carts, old tires and sunken lumber out of the water. Each year more volunteers showed up for the annual blitz. In 1994 even the Lieutenant Governor Yvon Dumont built a raft, rolled up his jean cuffs, and took to the water to help in the cleanup. S.O.S. is now working toward restoration of the river bottom forest running along its banks and looking at environmentally friendly ways to make the river usable for recreation.

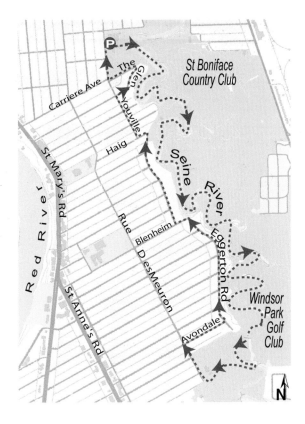

The riverbanks are a unique habitat. Large Manitoba maple, green and black ash, American elm, plains cottonwood, basswood and sandbar willow stand with their undergrowth of ostrich ferns and wood nettle. The uplands edges of the flood plains forest merge with bur oak, big bluestem, high bush cranberry, American hazelnut, saskatoon, snowberry, wild rose and wild red raspberry.

LaSalle River

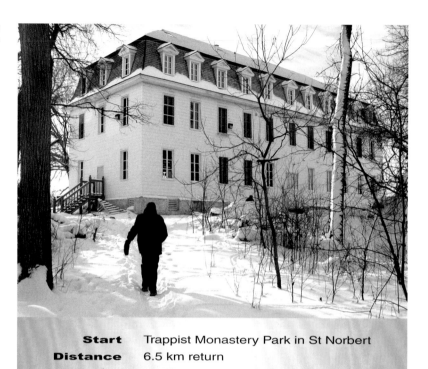

Start Trappist Monastery Park in St Norbert

Distance 6.5 km return

We have snowmobilers to thank for this snow-packed pathway on the frozen La Salle River. Our route begins at the Trappist Monastery Historical Park and follows the river to St. Norbert Provincial Heritage Park where the LaSalle flows into the Red River.

The LaSalle is a lovely winding river bordered by thick groves of trees. Spots of evergreen and the red bark of dogwood add welcome colour to a world of white. Here and there, matted grass hangs from branches high above as evidence of the height of the river during spring flood.

Trappist Monastery Historical Park - Remains of the tyndall stone chapel and monastery - 'the Ruins', date back to 1892 when the Trappist Order of Monks became established here. At one time, they ran a thriving agricultural operation with 37 priests busily engaged in tending bees and milking cows. They were completely cut off from the rest of the world, and the isolation of the place was vitally important to these monks. Over time this seclusion became threatened by encroaching development, and in 1978 the Trappists decided to move to more remote southwestern Manitoba. Subsequently, the citizens of St. Norbert worked to preserve this site, and even though the vacant chapel and residential wing were gutted by fire in 1983, the restored ruins became a provincial heritage park in 1987.

St Norbert Arts and Cultural Centre now occupies

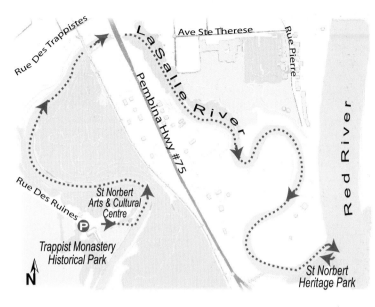

the four storey Guest House built by the Trappists in 1912. This eye-catching building with its dormer windows, 12 foot ceilings, and gleaming hardwood floors, has been declared a provincial heritage site.

The city has now acquired, as park space, 121 acres of forest on the south bank of the river. For years, this natural wooded area has been a favourite of local residents who like to ski and ride horses through the park. Over time, the city plans to build an 8 km nature walk from the forks of the Red and Seine rivers all the way to LaBarrier Park.

St. Norbert Heritage Park

When you reach the mouth of the LaSalle, climb up the high bank for a memorable view of the river and to reach the park. St Norbert Heritage Park gives us a glimpse of how people lived here 125 years ago. There are five houses that date back to the time of the Red River Resistance. The Park was designed to illustrate how a natural landscape, once used for hunting, fishing and camping by Native peoples, evolved into a French-speaking Metis settlement, and then a French agricultural community.

Another development planned for the park is the reconstruction of an early Indian camp site The region near the mouth of the LaSalle River may have been occupied by human beings as early as 6000 B.C. An ancient Palaeo Indian spearhead was found near a small stream that flows into the LaSalle at St. Norbert. This artifact, made of a type of stone that occurs naturally in the Canadian Shield, probably represents the seasonal movement of hunters from the forest to the grassland to hunt buffalo.